The Fragrance of Pure Love

Swamini Krishnamrita Prana

Mata Amritanandamayi Center
San Ramon, California, United States

The Fragrance of Pure Love
by Swamini Krishnamrita Prana

Published by:
    Mata Amritanandamayi Center
    P.O. Box 613
    San Ramon, CA 94583-0613 USA
    Tel: (510) 537-9417

First edition by MA Center: 2013

Copyright © 2013 by Mata Amritanandamayi Center, San Ramon, California, USA

All rights reserved No part of this publication may be stored in a retrieval system, transmitted, reproduced, transcribed or translated into any language, in any form, by any means without the prior agreement and written permission of the publisher.

In India:
    www.amritapuri.org
    inform@amritapuri.org

In USA:
    www.amma.org

In Europe:
    www.amma-europe.org

Contents

1. Finding a Home with God — 7
2. A Childhood of Mangoes and Bliss — 15
3. Born to Uplift Humanity — 23
4. The Guru Guides Us to God — 29
5. On the Trail of True Beauty — 37
6. Mother of Understanding — 43
7. The Fragrance of Love — 49
8. The Love of a Perfect Master — 55
9. Transforming Stones into Gold — 63
10. Seva – The Alchemy of Love — 69
11. A River of Love — 75
12. She Who Brings the Rain — 83
13. From Grass to Milk — 91
14. Bowing Down to all of Creation — 97
15. Perfect Surrender — 103
16. The Flow of Grace — 111
17. Guiding Our Footsteps — 117
18. Cultivating Innocent Faith — 123

"You have no idea how hard I've
looked for a gift to bring You.
Nothing seemed right.
What's the point of bringing gold to the gold mine,
or water to the ocean?
Everything I came up with
was like taking spices to the Orient.
It's no good giving my heart and my soul
because You already have these.
So I've brought You a mirror.
Look at Yourself
and remember me."

— Rumi

Chapter 1

Finding a Home with God

The first time I saw Amma in 1982, She was sitting inside a small thatched hut made of coconut leaves, engaged in conversation with a few people seated on the floor around Her. When I walked inside Amma jumped up and came over to greet me with a welcoming embrace. Her overflowing love took my breath away. I was almost in shock, as I had never imagined anyone giving so much love to a stranger.

I had just come from a spiritual centre in northern India, where the Guru sat at a comfortable distance and no one was allowed to touch him. Some spiritual teachers feel that their energy can be taken away through another's touch. It is said that energy flows down the body and out through the feet. When the feet are reverentially touched, one can receive a blessing. To protect their energy many teachers do not allow any physical contact, but only prostrations from a distance.

Amma was way beyond all of this. In Her compassion, She enthusiastically offered Her body, life and soul to the world. She was just unbelievable, to my 'spiritually educated' mind. I thought I knew everything about spirituality but Amma quickly showed me that I did not know anything about pure Divine Love. I was astonished by the love and affection that so spontaneously emanated from Her.

Luckily for me, grace manifested giving me the opportunity to stay with Amma in Her ashram at a time when there were only fourteen residents.

Living with Amma opened up a whole new realm of devotion where my mind could be channeled in a useful direction, away from the world. Spiritual teachings that I had only read or heard about became a direct experience before my very eyes, manifesting through Amma's life and actions . At the same time, She was always so humble. Her humility is amongst Her most profound yet subtlest teachings.

Her actions were difficult for me to comprehend at first, as I had never seen anyone so God-intoxicated. Occasionally She would lie down on the sand or sometimes on one of our laps, singing songs to God or just silently drifting in a divinely intoxicated state, laughing or crying with ecstasy.

Amma guided us in daily spiritual practices, encouraging us to choose a form of the Divine, apart from Herself, as our focus for meditation. In order to increase our devotion and to develop our thirst and longing for union with the Divine, we needed to yearn for a form that we did *not* already have. Fortunately for us, Amma's form was so easy to attain. She made Herself available to whoever sought Her company, everyday for hours on end, even throughout the night.

At one point we decided to build Amma a small house to give Her more privacy; otherwise She was continually on call, at the mercy of anyone and everyone twenty-four hours a day. Two small rooms were constructed upstairs for Amma to live in: one for sleeping, the other for receiving visitors. We used the downstairs room for meditation. For the first few months after the building was completed, Amma refused to move from Her small hut as She felt that these two new rooms were far too fancy for Her. In fact, they were extremely plain. Eventually, due to our persistent pleading, Amma surrendered and moved in.

Every day we would gather in the room downstairs and sit for our meditation. One day, one of the *brahmacharis* (celibate male disciples) started to practice a special yoga asana that I had never seen before. Eyes wide open, I watched intrigued, as he sucked in his stomach until it became completely concave. I was astonished that the body could even do something like that!

I thought, 'Oh my goodness! What is going on here?' As I stared in shock at his disappearing stomach, Amma walked inside, saw me gaping and announced, "The girls will sit outside from now on."

From then on we few girls began to sit outside of the meditation hall on the verandah. It was much nicer to be outside with a view of the coconut trees, expanses of sand and the

Finding a Home with God

backwaters. There, outside with nature, I used to imagine Sri Krishna dancing just out of my reach – as the raindrops fell from the sky to the earth.

I learned how imagination can be one of the greatest gifts to guide us through long periods of meditation. It is difficult to gain concentration and to hold onto it for very long but when we use our imagination in a positive way, it can take us higher and higher in spirituality.

Life was blissful with Amma, unlike anything I had ever experienced before or could have even imagined existed. Still, there were challenging times as well.

Although the joy of spiritual life is unique, there is a term in spirituality known as 'the dark night of the soul.' It is a stage when one feels intense anguish, as if wedged between the pull of worldly life and a desire for spiritual life. The pain occurs because we have not yet embraced spiritual life completely. During this time we know that there is no other path but the spiritual journey, yet we still somehow feel pulled towards the world and this causes intense suffering.

During my first few years with Amma, I felt that I went through something like this. I remember being too embarrassed to tell anyone. I thought I was the only one going through this and I felt terrible because I believed that no one else could feel that low or have such dreadful feelings. When I finally admitted to another one of the western residents what I was going through, he told me that he too had experienced exactly the same thing during the initial two years he spent with his first Guru. Realizing that this 'dark night' was not uncommon to spiritual seekers helped me to move beyond it.

Amma reveals that true faith can never be shaken. If it is, then that is not *real* faith. The good thing is that once we have passed through this stage, our faith in God can never be lost. It is a common experience that the first two years of living full time in an ashram are the hardest times of all because one has to make all sorts of adjustments to a new way of life.

Amma reminds us that we are not isolated islands; everyone is like a link in the same chain. We are all going to experience much of the same things in life, just in slightly different ways.

Amma's advice to me at this time of suffering was that I had to develop either an attachment towards Amma or an attachment towards the ashram. Amazingly, I chose the ashram.

I had come to live with Amma for Her to guide me as my Guru. It seemed that almost everyone else had come to live at the ashram for Amma to be their Mother. They therefore had much more of a loving maternal closeness with Her than I did. For me, who looked upon Amma primarily as my Guru, there was a bit of a distance. Along with love, I felt a reverential fear towards Amma because I saw Her mainly as my Guru, so I felt it was easier to create a bond of attachment with the ashram. Years later I learnt that the aspect of *'bhaya bhakti'* (reverential fear) is a necessary part of devotion that prevents us from behaving too casually with the Guru.

During my first ten years at the ashram I travelled with Amma wherever She went. When the number of people travelling with us began to grow, I felt it was better to stay back and help with the upkeep of the ever expanding ashram. I thought I would be more useful at the ashram doing some work there, rather than travelling with Amma and hundreds of people. After all, to me, the ashram *was* just like Amma. It is said that the ashram is the body of the Guru and that is truly how I have always felt.

Most people love being in Amma's physical presence, but they do not necessarily feel the same towards the ashram. I started off the other way, by feeling a firm commitment towards the ashram. With a profound grace unfolding, I ended up getting the chance to move closely with Amma as well.

Amma knew I was the type of person to keep a little distance from Her, so She gradually pulled me closer and closer when She perceived the time was right. Perhaps She also felt it was time for Her to work on me a little more deeply.

I now have even more love for Amma than for the ashram, however, they really are one and the same. An ashram essentially *is* the Guru's body and Amritapuri is my heaven on earth.

Chapter 2

A Childhood of Mangoes and Bliss

Whenever we travel with Amma by car She invariably talks about Her childhood. Her face lights up with joy when She recalls how it was in the olden days. I sometimes wonder why She chooses to think of those days so often. Maybe it is because the values of selflessness and love were upheld to a much greater extent back then.

When Amma was growing up, traditional values formed the foundation of village and family life. She says that because everyone was so focused on giving and sharing they did not need any other spiritual practices. She fondly recalls Her youth over and over again in order to remind us to hold onto these core values of selflessness, love, giving, and sharing as our own foundation as well.

The Fragrance of Pure Love

Once when Amma was speaking to a devotee She described how Her mother used to work all the time. Her mother raised chickens, ducks, goats and cows. She tended to the small coconut trees and made rope from the fibre of the coconut husk. She planted lots of Ayurvedic medicinal herbs in the front yard, plucked the leaves of those plants and prepared remedies for the treatment of all sorts of ailments, everything from coughs and fever to swollen hands. Although uneducated, Amma's mother was an excellent businesswoman and often made twice as much money as her husband did. She was constantly working in addition to looking after her large family. Despite all the hard work, she was loving towards everyone. Her physical work was difficult, but in those days actions were performed with an attitude of worship and her mind was constantly focused on God.

When Amma's mother cooked food, she always *first* set some aside for the neighbours or anyone else who might be hungry. The initial thought was always to give to others. This selfless attitude just came naturally in those days. If guests arrived they were served the best food available and the children were given only rice water for their meal. In protest, the children sometimes stole curd or pieces of coconut, mixed it with sugar and ate it in secret together. If they were found out, they received a good scolding.

Amma was always ready to do anything to help when the guests arrived in Her home. Occasionally if there was no dry wood available, She would climb a coconut tree and pull off some dry leaves to make a fire for tea. Sometimes if Amma could not be found, Her mother would discover Her up in a coconut tree. She would then scold Her saying, "No one will marry you except a coconut tree climber!" Amma always quickly changed *that* subject.

If a marriage took place in the village, everyone helped out by offering gold jewelry or some money to ensure that the newlyweds were taken care of. In those days no one thought of hoarding for tomorrow, but always gave whatever they had.

People who are wealthy often feel they have the freedom to do anything they want. But if they lack the underlying values of selfless love and hard work with the proper attitude, then it will be very challenging for them to find true happiness. Today, good principles are dying away fast. In India and all over the world ancient values are quickly eroding.

Amma's whole culture and spiritual outlook is based on the values of giving and the joy that comes from that. She is trying to keep these values from dying out in the world by offering a perfect example for us to follow.

Amma exemplifies the ideals of pure selflessness in Her own life. She may tell others to take rest if they are sick, but She Herself will never do that. The majority of people usually try to make their lives easy by taking the fastest and most comfortable way out, thinking only of what they can take. Amma on the other hand, always remains on the traditional, purist path, never compromising Her values of love and compassion. She thinks only of what She can give.

Amma has always seen the wonder and beauty of God everywhere. Even when She was little, Amma knew that God was in everything: in the walls, the trees, the plants, the butterflies, in absolutely everything. She recalls how She used to chase the dragonflies, butterflies, bees and birds in the forest around Her home. Sometimes the bees and dragonflies would sting Her when She caught them, not realizing She just wanted to sing songs to them. She would make up songs spontaneously as She danced in bliss through the forest, telling stories to the trees and flowers. She spoke to all of nature as an intimate friend, because to Amma, it truly was.

When we are in the car and Amma sees a river, She recalls how all the children used to go swimming in the backwaters. If they were not allowed to swim, the girls would go into the river and hold their dresses above the knees. This way they could play in the water but still keep their clothes dry so that their mothers would not find out.

When Amma was small, if the wind blew strongly, She and all the other children would rush outside to the mango trees and pray fervently that the breeze would blow fruit to the ground. Today, just the sound of the wind in the trees reminds Amma of those innocent prayers.

In today's world the whole of creation is crying out for the healing touch of the Divine Mother – not only people, but also Mother Nature herself. When Amma was growing up, the deep connection the villagers had with nature allowed them to appreciate how Mother Nature is constantly giving to us so selflessly. Nowadays it is the opposite: our lack of reverence has led to the ongoing destruction of nature. In order to protect the world we live in, we need to re-establish the traditional values of care and respect towards all beings.

A few years back, on the island of Mauritius, Amma insisted on going to a particular residence in order to bless the house and the family who owned it. The family no longer lived there and the house was standing vacant. The rest of us felt it was totally unnecessary for Amma to go to all this trouble. Amma had just given darshan throughout the night and we wanted Her to get some rest. But She was adamant.

She wanted to return to the place where She had stayed years ago, so that She could say 'Thank you' to the trees and plants and to the walls of the house that had given Her shelter. She reminded us that we should never forget the foundation from which we have come and should always be thankful to it.

Chapter 3

Born to Uplift Humanity

Amma knew right from the beginning that Her life was meant to uplift suffering humanity. Her expressions of overflowing love started when She was just a young girl. Even then She felt compelled to try to alleviate the suffering of others in whatever way She could.

Amma sees God in all things. Because of this She spent a good deal of Her childhood in bliss. Although She also witnessed a lot of heart-breaking suffering due to the tremendous poverty in Her village.

Many of the villagers suffered intense physical pain because they could not afford to spend even a few rupees on pain medication. There were parents who had to pull their children out of school because they did not have enough money to buy even a single sheet of paper for their children's school examinations.

The small huts that most villagers lived in were made of woven coconut leaves and the roofs had to be remade every year, especially before the monsoon season. If the families could not afford this, the rain would often leak through the roofs. Mothers who had umbrellas would sit up all night holding them over their children to protect them from the heavy rain. If the fishermen failed to catch any fish, which was often the case, then those poor villagers did not eat.

Some husbands drowned their sorrows in alcohol, drinking and playing cards on the beach. Upon returning home, they beat their wives. Sometimes drunkards passing by would also create a disturbance. Knowing all of this, Amma always had the desire to find a way for all those people, especially the women, to have at least a small house with two rooms to protect them.

When She was a child, many elderly people came to Amma in distress. She naturally and spontaneously comforted them, letting them cry on Her shoulder or collapse on Her lap.

If their families lost interest in helping them, Amma would bring the neglected ones back home with Her to bathe them, feed them and clothe them properly.

In thinking of others, Amma forgot Herself and became like a river of love and compassion flowing to the destitute, transforming pain into hope, and creating a bright new future for so many.

Amma felt the daily pain of others as Her own pain. She never thought about whether they were male or female. She just spontaneously responded to the pain calling out to Her. She offered whatever food or money She had or could find and sometimes even stole from Her family in order to help others. This caused a tremendous strain on the family.

Amma's sister remembers: "Our mother never scolded Amma when She gave away food to the poor but Amma gave away practically *everything* we had! She'd go to visit people, come back home and take whatever they needed from our house. She gave them rice, vegetables, clothes, utensils, etc. We even worried about our bathing soap! In those days we saw it as

The Fragrance of Pure Love

theft. Sometimes I would go into the bathroom and throw away the soap that Amma had used for bathing the elderly, I was so disgusted and couldn't bear to use the same soap they had touched. We used to tell our mother about everything Amma was doing and She would get punished, even spanked. Only now do we understand it was charity born of unconditional love. I often apologize to Amma for everything we put Her through back then, not knowing Her Divine nature."

There were four daughters in the family and society, being what it was back then, imposed numerous stringent rules on women: Women should neither be seen nor heard. They must not speak loudly – not even the walls should hear them! The earth should not feel their footsteps. They should be quiet and respectful towards men and should never voice their opinions.

Amma and Her sisters were raised very strictly. Their mother told them they should not talk loudly, run or walk fast; they must wear only a very small dot on the forehead, not a large one; and they should never draw attention to themselves.

Out of Her compassion, Amma ignored the harsh regulations of Indian society. As She grew older, Her behaviour grew even more odd according to village standards. She broke free from the iron cage imposed upon women in that day. When She started giving darshan and embracing strangers, including men, Her family and the villagers were horrified. At this time many of the people Amma had helped for years cast Her aside. Her family was not to blame for their attitude of horror at Amma's behaviour. They were concerned because they wanted to get all four of their daughters married and they feared that Amma's unusual behaviour would bring shame to their family name.

How were they all to know that Amma's strange behaviour was simply a sign of Her greatness?

Back then, *sannyasis* (Hindu monks) often travelled from village to village, teaching people about spirituality. But Amma never saw a sannyasi in the local area until She was about twenty years old. She patiently accepted the ignorance of Her family and the villagers because She knew Her purpose and what the future would hold for Her.

The truth is: when a flower blossoms and exudes an exquisite beauty and fragrance, how can you keep the bees away?

Chapter 4

The Guru Guides Us to God

Amma does not just sit and talk about spirituality; She lives it every day, showing us a perfect example. Her actions are even more powerful than the messages in the scriptures. She is the living essence of all the scriptures. The holy story of Her life exemplifies all the paths of yoga: karma (selfless action), bhakti (devotion) and jnana (knowledge).

Amma reminds us that we are *destined* for Divinity and She tries to awaken the desire for eternal happiness within us. Through the Guru's actions we can see God in a tangible way. With Amma, Divine Love can be seen and felt as our *own* experience.

The whole cycle of our physical and spiritual evolution is perfectly planned. Therefore, we must learn to surrender, in order to go beyond our pain and reach that final state of union with the Divine. In truth, we create all our own problems through the negative attitude of our minds. Out of compassion, the Guru sets up situations that destroy this negativity and dismantle our ego, and slowly it is worn down.

A Spanish lady who did not understand English was visiting the ashram. She wanted to buy something sweet, so she went to the café where the menu is written entirely in English. She bought a piece of cake because it was advertised as 'without ego.' She felt that Amma was so compassionate to provide a cake without ego – even though the sign had actually said, 'without eggs'! We never know in which way She is working on us…

There is a poignant story about a devotee who attended the discourses of his spiritual Master every night. For the first full year, the teacher completely ignored this disciple even though the disciple always came to *satsang* (spiritual talks). Being ignored every day made the man feel extremely frustrated and even angry, but he still continued to attend the discourses keeping his anger under control.

During the second year at the beginning of the talk, the Master gestured for the disciple to come and sit in front of him. The man believed he might at last get some attention, but the Master continued to deliberately ignore him during the entire discourse.

As time went by, the disciple's anger was gradually replaced by a deepening sadness. Through this process the disciple's ego slowly melted and his mind became totally silent. One day when the disciple was feeling the absolute depth of his sadness, the Guru came close to him. He touched his disciple's face tenderly and looked deeply into his eyes. At that very moment the disciple became enlightened, by the grace of his patient and compassionate Master.

It is only when our ego starts to melt and we become nothing, that we start to become something. Amma says that only then will we truly begin to become a part of everything.

Every one of Amma's actions embodies Her teachings. We can study thousands of spiritual books and listen to hundreds of trendy teachers, but only the grace from one who has uncovered the deepest layers of the soul will guide us to the goal. Truly nothing else will.

Amma says it is not for Her to tell us everything; it is for us to learn from life. She has shared so many spiritual truths, again and again and again. She is a fountain of wisdom. We love to watch Her and listen to Her satsangs, but most of us think we know everything already. We have read all kinds of spiritual books about every possible traditional and modern form of spirituality. Yet, how many of us actually try to practice the spiritual principles?

In the tenth century, there lived a Grand Vizier of Persia, Abdul Kassem Ismael, who was so attached to his knowledge that he could not bear to be apart from his library of 117,000 books. When he travelled, a caravan of four hundred camels carried all of his books. The camels were trained to walk in the alphabetical order of the books they were carrying. This is a true story.

Even if we have all the knowledge of the world within us, it is hard to draw it forth at the correct moment. This is why we need a true Master like Amma to guide us.

The Guru Guides Us to God

On an Indian tour a few years ago, we were driving to the next program after having stopped for a roadside picnic with everyone. Amma was sitting on the floor in Her camper making an origami paper boat. There was a child with her and She told him to pay attention. She was trying to teach him how to make his own boat.

"Look closely," She said, as She folded each crease of the paper. She counted, "One, two, three, four…" as She folded the paper twelve times. It took that many folds to make the small paper boat. Looking on, I realized that this is exactly what the spiritual Master is doing for us, showing us how we can make each of our actions, one by one, into a beautiful creation – maybe even into a boat that will sail us across the ocean of *samsara* (the cycle of life and death)!

Amma repeated the steps twice for the little boy but in the end he only wanted to play with the boat. He was not so interested in learning how to make one. We are also like this in many ways, far more eager to find a way to enjoy ourselves and play, than to take the time and have the patience to learn the lessons that life presents to us. Luckily, Amma is patiently waiting for us until we are ready to learn.

Amma is known for Her tremendous love, but I think Her capacity for showing patience is even more phenomenal. She just keeps on demonstrating through Her every action, what the scriptures are trying to convey to us.

Only a God-realized soul knows the most important spiritual concepts that can help us along the path. We must choose very carefully when accepting a spiritual Master and never settle for anything less than someone who has realized the Supreme Truth. There are very few such people around. Sometimes we hesitate to approach them and are afraid to come close to them, knowing they will see our bare, ugly, selfish thoughts and past deeds. Yet their minds are so pure and their love so all-encompassing that when they look at us, they see only the mistakes of an innocent child.

Some people fall so madly in love with Amma that they ask Her if they should leave their worldly life and go to live at the ashram in India. Usually Amma's answer to them is that there is nothing wrong with the life of a householder, as long as you keep the ultimate goal in mind. Amma says that wherever we go, we should remember to keep a small space inside of us for our real home: our real home with God.

Chapter 5

On the Trail of True Beauty

Beauty has become something we do to ourselves, something we put on from the outside, almost like a mask. Amma exemplifies how true beauty radiates from within.

Amma says, "It is *selflessness* that allows our beauty to shine forth, past the shell of the ego." Her beauty lies not only in what She shares with us when we are with Her, but also in the subtle layers of unspoken thoughts and feelings She inspires in us. The more we express love and concern towards others, the purer our hearts become and the sweeter our fragrance.

Amma is like a perfume factory where the world's most exquisite fragrances are created and I am just lucky enough to have been given a job in Her factory, so a little of the fragrance has rubbed off on me, as it surely has on others as well.

When we travel, all types of people are deeply moved by Amma's divine energy – the airline staff, cleaning ladies, security staff and various other passengers and airport personnel, many of whom have never had the chance to receive Amma's darshan. On one occasion when we were leaving India, a large group of policemen on security duty came to escort Amma to the plane, as they usually do. This security is quite unnecessary but it seems to be the policemen's favourite job, as they all vie with each other to get close and walk next to Amma.

Wherever we go they surround Amma trying to protect Her from the crowd, even when there is no one there! Although I usually walk with Amma when we travel, they do not have me on their list of important people to escort and often find me quite invisible. Sometimes I have to fight my way through them to catch up with Amma. She will often wait for me, but sometimes I just cannot keep up with Her.

One time the policemen were very happy to whisk Amma away and leave me behind to

On the Trail of True Beauty

collect our bags at the metal detector. I was trying to catch up but ended up a few minutes behind. Luckily for me, Amma had left a trail to follow, a trail of happy, blissed-out people. All along the way I kept coming across people bubbling over with joy, so I could tell exactly in which direction Amma had gone!

I am usually with Amma as we make our way quickly through the crowd, so I get to see the excitement when people greet Amma, but I miss out on seeing the lasting effects of this encounter. Walking by myself on that day, I had time to notice the ecstasy She gifted to all of those who came into contact with Her. It was like experiencing a wave of joy in Her wake!

Amma is able to inspire us not only with Her darshan, but also simply with a glance, a smile or a touch. Amma's joy flows to us purely by our being in Her presence.

One morning at a *Brahmasthanam* (temple with four-sided Deity designed by Amma) program in Bangalore, Amma told the devotees to imagine pouring curd, ghee, and rosewater on the feet of their beloved Deity. While everyone had their eyes closed and were deep in

The Fragrance of Pure Love

contemplation, Amma took a rose that was lying next to Her on the *peetham* (raised platform the Guru sits on) and moved it across to the other side of Her, putting it down to exemplify placing a rose on the feet of our beloved Deity.

Only one young lady in the audience had her eyes open. Instead of closing her eyes, she was gazing up at Amma in rapture. She held a small, sleeping child nestled over her shoulder. Amma's mischievous glance connected with her, and her face lit up with joy. It was such an endearing smile that Amma gave, and that young woman was the only person in the entire audience who saw it. She squeezed her child in excitement and closed her eyes in bliss for a few seconds. Then she opened her eyes again and beamed, overflowing with effervescent joy.

I noticed this exchange and was also caught in the rapturous moment of seeing Amma shoot an arrow directly into someone's heart. She helped that devotee to experience the deep bliss lying within her Self. I felt so happy that this young mother was able to share such a personal and heart-warming moment with Amma. She probably had to sacrifice a great deal just to be able to see Amma, even for this one program.

The woman's joy was beautiful for me to see. I experienced almost as much happiness as she did! We should try to experience our own joy through other people's happiness. We do not even have to be the one going for darshan; we can share the experience and feel that same joy simply by being in Amma's presence and watching the effect She has on all those around Her. Amma finds a way to open up everyone's heart in one way or another.

Amma spends every second of Her existence seeing the beauty and true reality of everything. She sees the existence of Divinity in everyone and everything and is trying Her utmost to share that vision with us. She wants only the best for us, to take us to that place where She dwells, and to help us to experience the same reality that She does. This is why Amma is so beautiful – because Her compassion shines through every glance. Her eyes are always sparkling with Divine light.

Chapter 6

Mother of Understanding

Amma looks deeply at every person who comes to Her. She sees that their ego and their problems have only developed from the pain they experienced somewhere in their past. While we might dismiss a certain person as annoying or frustrating, Amma instead, gives love, which melts away their pain. That is the beauty of who She is and what She is offering us. She understands us more deeply than we can ever comprehend.

On my fiftieth birthday we were travelling to a program when Amma suddenly turned to me and asked, "What is the date today?" I said that I did not know. Amma asked Swamiji. He also had no idea. I asked the driver, and he told the date. "Oh!" I exclaimed… It just slipped out.

The Fragrance of Pure Love

Amma asked what the matter was. I replied, "Amma, it's my fiftieth birthday today, I hadn't realized." Later some people found out that it was my birthday and arranged for a cake and a special birthday darshan. It was a beautiful surprise and experience at the time, but celebrating my birthday is something I would never usually do. Monastics are not really supposed to celebrate birthdays, and I would never intentionally remind Amma that it was my birthday. Now, to my complete horror, it seems as though everyone knows my birthdate!

A couple of years later, a few people decided they would again arrange a birthday celebration for me. Knowing this might happen, I told them repeatedly beforehand, that I did not want them to arrange anything special on that day.

But people get caught up in the birthday spirit. A cake was prepared and I was told to go up to Amma for darshan. I was so mad when I found out about this and refused to go to the stage. It was an extremely busy day for Amma, with a huge crowd at the program. These birthday troublemakers went to the stage to ask Amma if She would call for me. Amma looked strangely at them, and remarked, "I don't know if she will like that type of thing, you should tell her that she doesn't have to come if she doesn't want to."

When they brought back the news of what Amma had said I felt extremely happy. It reminded me that there is at least *one* person who truly understands me. Amma knew my feelings about celebrating birthdays. That was the greatest gift I could have ever received, to know that Amma genuinely understands me, even when no one else does.

Amma is the Mother of us all, accepting and nurturing everybody and truly caring for all beings equally. She listens to every detail and acknowledges every aspect of a person and their feelings, the ones they are conscious of as well as the deep underlying subconscious ones.

Occasionally when Amma starts a satsang story, we might think, 'Oh I've heard that story before.' Still, if we are open and have awareness, we can understand things on a different level each time we hear it. Sometimes it takes years to realize that Amma is responding to something inside of us that is so much deeper than we could have ever imagined; much deeper than the superficial layers we usually dwell in.

Amma understands people better than their own parents do. Parents may love their children, but it does not mean they truly understand them. I know of one young teenager who had an unfulfilled desire. He had pierced his ears with small earrings but he wanted to get a bigger pair that was more fashionable. He asked his mother and father if he could get a larger pair of earrings.

They said, "No, definitely not." They were totally against the idea. Then one day he went to Amma for darshan and She said to him, "Oh, very nice earrings, but don't you think a slightly larger size would be better for you?" This boy happily went back to tell his parents, "See, Amma understands me better than you ever understand me!"

Amma was in tune with him and his desires. This happens all the time, because Amma is one with the essence of who we truly are. Because She knows Herself, She knows who we are too. We do not know who we really are at all. All we know are the thoughts and the emotions

Mother of Understanding

that always cloud our mind. These take us over and say, 'This is who you are: you're too fat or too thin; you're too dark or too light; you've got the wrong hair colour…' Amma knows who we really are, more deeply than we know ourselves, right down to our very cell structure. Never doubt that.

There are seventeen thousand students studying in Amma's university in India. On one occasion one of the students staying in the hostel told the other students, "It's just like a jail here; we can't do anything fun, it's like a jail." The very next time he went to Amma for darshan, Amma asked him, "How's the jail?" Just of Her own accord She brought up the subject to him.

He was stunned, totally stunned, that Amma could understand his mindset. It completely changed things for him and after that he was able to adjust himself to all the rules. He knew there really was somewhere he could always go where someone would completely understand him, more than his parents, even more than his best friends.

Amma embraces and receives every part of us, right through the deepest layers of our darkest shadows. She understands us better than we can understand ourselves. She sees and accepts us entirely, hearing all of our thoughts and desires, without any projections affecting Her perceptions, because She is detached and not thinking of Her own feelings. She reaches the depths of our purest soul, allowing that most beautiful part of us to glimpse the light of day.

Chapter 7

The Fragrance of Love

Amma loves us more than we could ever possibly imagine. She reaches out to us while reminding, "There is a voice crying out in everyone to feel the sweetness of pure love, but it remains unheard. We are born to experience pure love, and our wealth is to experience pure love, but it is truly the rarest commodity, the experience of pure love in this world." Amma gives us hope by coming to answer that voice crying out in us. She gives the love we are genuinely yearning for.

I remember one time while we were travelling in India, a devotee who was suffering from cancer was on the phone talking with Amma. She was starting to quietly cry a little, so the devotee was trying to cheer Her up on the other end of the phone. Yet still She shed tears. The devotee kept on saying, "It's okay Amma. I feel Your grace. It's okay."

When they had finished talking on the phone, Amma still had tears in Her eyes. I was sitting next to Her thinking to myself, 'Why is Amma feeling so sad? She knows the truth: that this body is not eternal.' I said to Her, "Amma, you know the truth…"

There I was, giving Amma a little reminder speech on Vedanta. Amma looked at me and replied, "I know… *but I feel their pain!*"

That kept me quiet for awhile. I felt so ashamed of myself. I went into my own experience of contemplation, how Amma's greatness is not only in achieving the state of God-realization, but going way beyond that to encompass a life of such compassion that She sees everyone everywhere as a mirror of Herself.

Sitting in the car in silence in the dark, I then became the one silently shedding tears.

Looking at Amma, I was reminded of a shooting star of compassion, travelling beyond the limit of everything and coming back down to earth, to our level in order to fulfill our wishes, with blessings. She is trying to teach us to live a life of compassion.

The Fragrance of Love

One night at the end of a Brahmasthanam program in Mangalore, a devotee was waiting for Amma amidst all the others. Amma had not slept at all. She had just enough time to bathe and change Her clothes before we had to leave for the next program. We had a long drive ahead of us to Hyderabad.

This devotee had been crying for some time. He had been working around the clock for the three days of programs, doing *seva* (service) by arranging accommodations for all the devotees flocking to see Amma. He had not been able to come in for the program as the police had locked the ashram gates due to the large size of the crowds. Thinking that he had missed Amma's darshan he was crying in great distress.

When the devotees told Her that he had been working so hard and missed Her darshan, Amma forgot Her own exhaustion and pain and rushed towards him, giving a wonderful embrace and holding him close for a long time.

He ended up losing consciousness because he was so overwhelmed with Amma's love and compassion for him. When he passed out, Amma sat down on the steps holding him, calling out for someone to bring him some coconut water. He wanted to get up, but She insisted that he wait to drink the coconut water first. He could not believe his luck or the compassion of Amma to give him such a long embrace.

I then realized, that this is probably why Amma is only able to give some people in India just one second of darshan. Because if they had more, like this man, then it could prove to be too much for them! In just one second, Amma can give absolutely everything to us.

Just as Kuchela was allowed to offer Sri Krishna only one mouthful of puffed rice, we too need only one second of Amma's darshan to have the pathway of devotion unfold before us. A path lined with all the spiritual wealth that life can offer us.

Tradition says that Radha saw Sri Krishna only one time, by the Yamuna River. From that time onward She always loved Him and connected with Him through Her heart. Even though we may have only one darshan with Amma, She will never forget us and will always love us deeply, through all of eternity.

The Fragrance of Love

Amma says, "Unless your heart can melt with compassion for others, you'll never realize the truth of what the word 'Love' really means; it will just be a word in the dictionary." We must learn to open our heart like Amma does. There are no boundaries with Her. She melts into everyone. There is nothing separate from Her.

If we can relate to the suffering of others and rejoice in their happiness…see the joy in someone else's darshan as if it were our own, then our path to heaven will be paved with rose petals. It is a very difficult thing to do. This is why Amma reminds us constantly, "We are always beginners."

Amma is a flow of love. She gives Her best effort to pour as much love and attention as She can onto everyone, everyday. Amma is a Goddess amongst us, living closely with us as an ordinary human being, but loving all of us in an extraordinarily supernatural way.

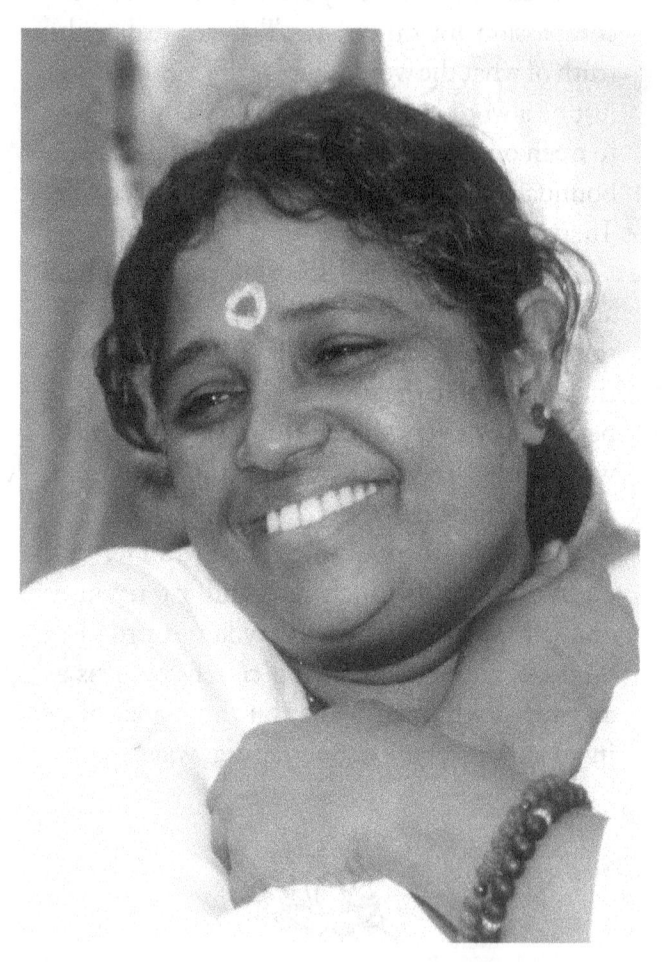

Chapter 8

The Love of a Perfect Master

The most powerful force on this earth is the love a God-realized soul has for us. They love us so purely, wanting nothing for themselves. They sacrifice their lives to set us free. Nowhere, absolutely nowhere, in the whole world are we ever going to find anything more beautiful, more giving and more trusting, than the love that a perfect Master has for us.

When Lord Buddha attained enlightenment, it was said that He never wanted to leave that blissful state. But as soon as He lay His palm upon the ground, the earth pleaded on behalf of every embodied soul, for Him to teach all beings the way out of misery. What could Lord Buddha do but return?

This is true love, love so sincere and genuine that most of us rarely come across it, even in our dreams. Very few of us are lucky enough to experience this kind of love in our waking state. We are seldom ready, or even able, to receive this love, let alone give it.

It is said that the greatest sacrifice for a Mahatma is to come down to this earth and live amongst us in all our unconsciousness. But that is the sacrifice they are ready to make.

When He was young, Lord Buddha had some enemies that were extremely jealous and wanted to discredit him. They sent Him the most famous courtesan of their time. Buddha loved her as He loved everyone, but He looked upon her with a fatherly love.

Though the courtesan was very beautiful, her mind was no longer innocent. She tried to offer herself to Lord Buddha. With a divine purity He smiled back at her. He rejected her romantic advances saying, "I will love you when no one else loves you. I will love you when every other love has abandoned you." At this, she grew angry and left.

The Love of a Perfect Master

Forty years later Buddha was nearing His death. He was being carried on a wooden stretcher to His final resting place when He saw a figure clothed in rags, crouched down against a nearby wall. It was a leper, a woman, an old hunchback with half her face eaten away.

Buddha told the attendants carrying Him to stop. He slowly dismounted from the stretcher and walked over to the woman. He wrapped His arms around her quietly in a loving embrace and reminded her, that He had said He would *always* love her.

This is the kind of love that Amma has for us: a universal love that goes way beyond any barriers. She is constantly reminding us through all Her actions, that She will always be there to love and protect us.

Amma comes down to our level and pretends to be like us in order to take us higher. It is a Divine play. Amma does not have to put Herself through the trouble of doing all the things She does for us: coming out every day, again and again, no matter how She feels; offering Herself to us in every possible way. If we look at any great

Guru in history, can we find even one who has done nearly as much? I don't think so.

Amma's love, that maternal love She has for us, never tires of taking the time and effort to guide us, to entertain us and to sing beautiful bhajans for us. If we cannot imbibe Her teachings through the thoughts and words that She shares during satsang or one on one, we can learn through Her bhajans or by watching Her actions.

One year in Calcutta, at the end of the darshan program, Amma decided that She would go out on the streets and pick up rubbish, helping in the Amala Bharatam Campaign to clean up India.

Limited by an intense schedule, Amma is rarely able to go out and personally participate in Her many service projects, but on this occasion, the program finished just after ten p.m., which was early for Amma. Even though She had just sat for eleven hours straight giving darshan, She used Her night off to march out enthusiastically and join the team of dedicated sevites ready to clean the streets of Calcutta. At the end of a long day, this is how She wanted

The Love of a Perfect Master

to take Her rest and relaxation: collecting trash from the road.

Armed with gloves and masks, we walked out onto the dimly lit road. Most people's hearts were beating fast, with a mixture of the thrill and joy of selfless service and a touch of fear at what we might uncover, while diving into all the years of built up muck that thickly lined the streets.

When we reached the designated spot to start cleaning, Amma was quick to crouch down and pick up the rubbish, shoveling the filth into sacks that were loaded onto a truck. She mentioned to me that I should stay with Her. All my grand plans of diving into the waste were dashed, as I realized that I should keep at least one hand clean to be able to keep Amma's sari from trailing in the mud and filth, and to help Her up from sitting on the ground.

What totally surprised me was that every time I went to try and help Amma stand up, She had already shot straight up by Herself, without needing any help at all! I was absolutely shocked. She stood up so fast, just like an athlete might have done.

The Fragrance of Pure Love

I contemplated how stiff and sore Her leg muscles must have been from spending hours sitting cross-legged on the stage giving satsang, bhajans, and then darshan for the whole day and evening without the chance to move at all, but this did not seem to be the case.

I tried to concentrate a bit harder, so I could be quicker and reach in time to help Her stand up, but no matter how hard I tried, I was just not fast enough to be able to help at all.

It really showed me the incredible power and energy that true love can generate, if we have an attitude of dedication and awareness. Amma always shows us by Her acts of service and in so many other ways, that we too can become a powerhouse of energy, if we really try. Amma says, "When there is true love, there is no effort." She is a living example of these words.

When we watch Her we can see that *everything* Amma does is an embodiment of Her love and compassion for us. This is what She is showing us when She sits for darshan without getting up, sometimes for more than twenty-five hours in a row. She embraces everyone who comes to Her, no matter who it is, no matter what time or place. She relates to people as their confidant, listening to their stories, complaints, sorrows, and problems. It does not matter if She is tired or sick. She still always makes time for others, putting their needs before Her own.

Everything that a perfect Master does is entirely for *our* benefit. They have nothing to gain for themselves. Amma's wish is that She can offer Her life, in whatever way possible, to bring a taste of happiness and peace of mind to others.

Chapter 9

Transforming Stones into Gold

We are given many blessings in life, so much good advice and guidance, especially from Amma. She is showering us with grace all the time, but despite this we are often slow to change. Her patience is incredible, as She waits for us to transform ourselves. *Mahatmas* (Great Souls) come to this world to inspire us to grow. They live their lives setting the greatest example for us, but they will not force us to improve — that we must do ourselves.

When Mahatmas consecrate a temple, they imbue a living force into the stone idol by their *sankalpa* (divine resolve) and their breath. When Amma performs *Pratishta* (consecration) ceremonies, She infuses an inert stone with *Pranic* (energy) life force. At these times everyone can feel the powerful vibrations in the atmosphere and we have the opportunity to feel how extremely influential Amma's energy is.

It is sad to think an inert stone is so much more receptive to imbibe Amma's blessings than we humans are. She offers us that same energy every time She gives us darshan, but how slow we are to change.

Life will not be as patient with us as Amma is and will try to make us change faster. This is why pain comes into our lives: to *force us* to grow. We cannot always make the pain go away; instead we have to try to convert our suffering into something positive. Amma helps us to find the inherent strength inside of us to cope with anything. She dispels the darkness by shining the light of love and awareness on us.

While we were at a program in New York a few years ago, a local devotee told me an amazing story that happened to her daughter. The mother was very devoted to Amma, but her two children were not. In fact they thought their mother was quite strange to love Amma so much. Reluctantly, they came to attend the program in New York, just to please their mother.

Transforming Stones into Gold

Sadly, the daughter had her purse stolen while she was sitting in the crowd. She was extremely upset as it had a lot of money in it. She thought the culprit was a homeless man who had been sitting near her, but she could not prove anything.

Her mother knew there was nothing they could do. She told her daughter to try to forget about it and they went their separate ways for some time. After half an hour, the daughter found her mother again and was bubbling over with excitement.

She said, "Mum, you are not going to believe what happened just now!" She went on to explain that when she had gone upstairs the homeless man had approached her. He had the purse in his hand and had given it back to her, apologizing for having taken it.

He told her that he had been sitting watching Amma, when all of a sudden She turned to him and told him that what he had done was wrong. He should return the purse, apologize, and never do anything like that again. He admitted that he felt his life was truly changed by this experience; and the daughter developed a new impression of Amma as well.

Amma teaches us how to build a strong foundation of values and good qualities. From this foundation we should develop some positive practices to follow: living by a value system that drives our intentions, decisions and actions. It is entirely up to us what we gain from Amma's presence; this will vary according to our attitude and actions.

One year in London it was incredibly cold at the Alexandra Palace hall where the program was being held. A devotee was sitting down on a chair wearing a warm woolen shawl, but she was still cold and shivering. A young girl sitting next to her was wearing even less than she was and it was obvious that the girl was absolutely freezing.

This devotee thought to herself, 'She's colder than I am…I really should lend her my shawl,' but she was frozen herself. In the end, the compassion in her won. She removed her shawl and placed it around the girl's shoulders. At this point, they both stopped shivering.

Transforming Stones into Gold

For the rest of the night they both remained warm. The girl tried to give back the shawl every twenty minutes, as she felt quite guilty, thinking the other girl must surely be freezing, but the devotee was not feeling the cold anymore.

We have the power inside of us to change ourselves and our world. When we decide to do good actions, even if our attitude is still not the best, we begin to create the power of change inside ourselves and consequently, grace will surely flow.

People come to a Mahatma expecting all kinds of miracles for themselves and for the world – they expect them to be like a superhero casting a web of enchantment, to completely change everything. And yet, Mahatmas like Amma, truly *are* superheroes! She zaps us with the inspiration to help us walk on the path of truth and *dharma* (righteous action). She cannot walk our steps for us, but is forever encouraging us to go in the right direction, providing instructions when we veer on the wrong path. Amma offers us a map that will take us to the ultimate goal of God-realization.

Every word and action that Amma performs is intended to inspire us to do good actions. These positive actions will create good *karma* (chain of effect) and negate some of the suffering that we might be forced to experience due to our poor choices in the past. Amma's presence instills in us traditional values that cannot be learnt so easily in today's world. She inspires us to do good in order to reach our full potential as human beings.

Chapter 10

Seva – The Alchemy of Love

Anyone who watches Amma giving darshan might think that Amma needs a lot of people around Her helping; but in truth, She offers us the chance to serve, so *we ourselves* might learn. She lets us serve, entirely as an act of grace, to help us gain awareness and not at all because She needs any help. She is able to do everything perfectly well by Herself.

Occasionally, Amma may go on strike from letting us serve Her, just to teach us an important lesson. She might ban everyone from Her room, lock the door and decide to do everything Herself. She will cook Her own food, clean the room and wash Her clothes for a few days, in a fraction of the time it takes anyone else to do these tasks. This reminds us, it is not Amma who needs anything from us. We are the ones with many valuable lessons to learn.

Amma often reminds us, "It is not what we have been able to receive, but what we have been able to give that helps us experience the real beauty in life. If we simply take from the world, in the end we will become distant from our own true Self."

I read a story about a man whose wife had passed away eight years earlier. He went through a long period of depression and almost became suicidal. The only positive thing left in his life was the work he did as a doctor in his small medical clinic.

After seeing so many natural catastrophes on TV, he decided that he wanted to travel to some of the disaster stricken areas and offer his services. The fact that his wife was no longer alive and his children had all grown up allowed him to serve in this way. He travelled to impoverished communities where people had no access to health care and helped to set up twenty medical clinics. Eventually, these clinics were serving twenty-seven thousand patients every month. The doctor found that his state of depression completely disappeared and he experienced a new sense of accomplishment and purpose in his life. Now, fulfilling his new-found passion for service, he travels all over the world offering medical care wherever he is most needed.

Many of us feel burdened, angry or apathetic about the suffering we see in the world today, not knowing how to cope with it. This doctor realized that in helping other people, he receives back an even greater blessing than he gives: an enriched and satisfying life.

When we get completely caught up in the web created by our minds, it becomes hard to open up to the blessings life is continually showering upon us. We tend to become so lost in our own problems, we rarely consider the problems of others. Millions of people all around the world experience depression or some kind of mental anguish due to the loneliness of being cut off from family or friends. It is only through acts of service and compassionately helping others that we can escape the agony of our own mental suffering.

One day on tour, one of the volunteers came up to Amma and admitted he was going through an extremely difficult time. He told Amma it was his Saturn period and because of this he felt depressed and did not want to do seva anymore.

Amma laughed. She responded, "Saturn! What are you talking about? You have the presence of a Satguru. Even in the burning desert, under the shade of a tree, there is a coolness that can be felt. Son, you should still try to do seva, even if you don't feel like it!"

Do not blame the world and others for what we may have to suffer. We cannot always have the right attitude, but when we make ourselves do something good because we know that it is the right thing to do, even if we do not really want to, the flow of grace will come to us. All we can do is try to give our best effort.

Someone once wrote a morning prayer that we might all be able to relate to: "Dear God, so far today I have done alright. I have kept my mouth shut. I have not gossiped, yelled or lost my temper. I have not been greedy, grumpy, nasty, selfish or over-indulgent. I am glad about that. But in a few minutes, I am probably going to need a lot of help…because I am only, just now, getting out of bed!"

Seva – The Alchemy of Love

We should always try to do the right thing at the right time, in every moment, even if we do not feel motivated to do so. This is one of the best formulas for true success in any field, and will help us to reach the ultimate goal of Self-realization.

Amma tells us to be courageous and reminds us, "You are not little lambs. You are lion cubs, and you have infinite potential lying untapped inside of you." Recently, I overheard Amma advising someone, "One should be like a lion. When it walks through the forest, it goes some distance and then it turns around and looks back." She illustrated this point by turning Her head as She was saying it, and truly looked like an amazing lioness, powerfully looking back to see how far She had come.

She continued, "Even the tortoise when it is slowly plodding along, leaves a trail wherever it walks. We can be like this too in our lives, leaving some positive marks on the world. We should strive to leave behind something good."

We are lucky to so often be presented with the chance to do service. It is really one of the sweetest spiritual practices. The mind is constantly churning, trying to pull us down, but in the act of seva, in service, we can actively pour our energy into doing positive actions. This effort will re-train the negative habits of the mind. Do not stop to think whether you feel like it or not, because our feelings will be changing all the time. We have developed attachment to so many bad habits. Why not try to develop a new good habit instead?

Rather than living a mediocre existence, let us strive to cultivate an attitude of selflessness. It is not that one needs to do big important things, but all our small, kind and selfless actions can add up to something truly great.

Chapter 11

A River of Love

When Amma sees a need somewhere, She is always ready to fill it. This exemplifies what it means to tread the dharmic path of righteousness; we just have to try to do the right thing at the right time. Find out what we can do to help the world and use our skills to serve with love and awareness. It does not matter what we might do, it is the attitude behind the action that counts most.

A woman lived in the Swiss mountains about two hours away from Zurich by bus. Her husband had divorced and left, leaving her to raise their small child on her own. It was very difficult for her to make ends meet as she was quite poor and did not receive social security from the government.

The woman was a devout Catholic and always prayed to Mother Mary. She had heard that there were living saints in India but doubted she would ever get the chance to meet one. One day as she was walking past a restaurant she saw a flier about Amma's visit to Zurich. Feeling a strong desire to go and see Amma, she started saving money to be able to do so. She fasted for two days to save the money, but still fed her child.

She came down from the mountains, proceeded to the program site and waited to receive darshan. Not knowing English, let alone Amma's language, she realized there was no way to tell Amma about her problems. She cried quietly as she made her way towards Amma in the darshan queue.

Through her tears, she noticed a woman just a little ahead of her gave Amma some golden bangles when she went for darshan. She wished she too had something nice to offer. Amma was still wearing the bangles when it was her turn for darshan. She fell into Amma's lap, weeping and sobbing, but speechless. Amma looked at her very compassionately, took off the golden bangles and handed them to her. She then invited this distraught woman to sit close by Her side.

A River of Love

Amma turned to her and said, "Make sure that you do not sell these. You should pawn them so you can get some money to take care of your child. Don't worry; things will get better in the future."

Shocked and amazed, this lady went back to the mountains, pawned the bracelets and soon enough, with Amma's blessings, she received a job. The following year, the woman was able to get the pawned bracelets back, as she had gained control of her life and finances. She came down from the mountains when Amma returned. When she went for darshan, she joyfully placed the same gold bangles back on Amma's hands. For her, Amma is not only a saint, She is truly Divine.

Amma is always ready to serve. Like this, we too should be ready to dive in and help with a loving heart, in whatever way we can.

One night in Amritapuri after Amma had already sat for more than fifteen hours straight giving darshan, She came down from the stage and walked along the narrow pathway back to Her room. As She passed by the dining room, Amma could see through a gap in the devotees lining the pathway, that the sink in the dining area was extremely dirty. It was filthy and blocked with food. It needed to be cleaned, but no one had done it. She stopped, made Her way through the line of devotees, and started cleaning.

Even though She must have been exhausted, Amma was ready to set the right example for people through all of Her actions. Amma takes no time off. She is always on-duty, ready to teach us, in all kinds of situations.

When She started to clean the sink, suddenly people were ready to rush forward and help with this cleaning work, but She told everyone, "Don't just stand there looking at me. Go and clean the *other* sinks! Everyone wants to do *padapuja* (worship of the Guru's feet), but this is the *real* padapuja – the real worship of the Guru."

Not everyone may have the chance to wash the Guru's feet, but everyone has the chance of lovingly offering service to Her body through the acts of seva performed at any one of Amma's ashrams or programs. Any act of service performed

A River of Love

in remembrance of Her can become as holy as washing Her lotus feet.

Amma responds to the misery of the world by extending Herself every day to give whatever She can, no matter how She feels. With an open heart and enthusiasm, She moves forward, always giving Her maximum regardless of any obstacles She may encounter. She inspires all those around Her to do the same.

When the Amritapuri ashram was registered as a charitable institution in 1983, Amma said, "Do not make me like a caged parrot. Do not make this organization like a business firm. It should stand for the people, for the suffering humanity." Right from the very beginning, through all the years until this very day, that ideal has been absolutely and uncompromisingly upheld by Amma. She simply sees the needs of the people and acts.

Amma's organization, Embracing The World, has built over fifty schools in India and abroad, including a university with five campuses. It runs orphanages both in India and overseas. Amma started an initiative to curb farmer suicide, which is rampant in many parts of India. She gives fifty-nine thousand pensions to widows and the elderly and over forty-one thousand scholarships for poor students. She has dozens of hospitals and free medical clinics that provide medical care to the poor.

Embracing The World is often first on the scene at disasters all over the world. In 2004, during the Indian Tsunami, Amma transformed Her ashram in India into a refuge, feeding and looking after people who had lost their homes. Embracing The World was on the ground in 2005, during Hurricane Katrina; Amma donated one million dollars to relief funds. Amma also sent disaster relief teams to Japan during the Earthquake/Tsunami in 2011, providing food and bringing medical care to places no one else dared to go.

She has built over forty-five thousand houses for the homeless, with plans to build over one hundred thousand more. That means shelter for nearly one million people who had previously been homeless. She has directed people to plant thousands of trees and has fed millions of people all over the world…and so much more.

A River of Love

Amma inspires so much selflessness amongst Her children. Her charities are run on the volunteer services of thousands of people across the world. Even the poorest of the poor, when coming for darshan in India, often try to press a one rupee coin into Amma's hand. They cannot offer much more than this, but they also want to help because they know that She will use every rupee to serve others. Amma says they are like small birds making their offerings, and everything altogether becomes like the flow of a powerful river.

Amma's selflessness truly is Divine. She embraces crowds of people sometimes numbering in the tens of thousands, sitting till the very last person has been held. She does not think of Her own needs at this time.

We need not perform superhuman feats, only Amma can really do that, but if we just try to do something good and helpful every time the opportunity presents itself to us, then it will lead us out of our own sorrow towards the essence of pure love. There are so many takers in this world, but Amma is trying to teach us, through Her supreme example, how to become givers instead.

Chapter 12

She Who Brings the Rain

It is easy to declare our intention to do right actions, but we all know how hard it can be to put this into practice. It is the attitude and intention behind every action that really matters, not always the action itself. As long as we maintain a positive attitude, Amma will surely help us to overcome our negativities.

Amma shows us that if we have a positive attitude, the world becomes a truly beautiful place to live. Wherever Amma may be, She sees through the external world created by our egos and revels in the delightfulness of creation.

One Spring Amma visited Kenya to inaugurate Her new orphanage. As our car was leaving the airport, I rolled my window down so Amma could wave to the people who had come to welcome Her. Unfortunately the window got stuck and would not go back up again.

I felt nervous as I held our passports in my hand. I knew we were going to be driving through dangerous territory where someone could rob us through the window or even try to harm us in some way. As I was battling with the window control button, Amma looked at the rolled down window and remarked to me, "Big Problem!" When the driver started to apologize for the malfunctioning window, Amma immediately reassured him that it was fine. She *loves* to feel the breeze.

I laughed to myself at how quickly Amma had changed Her mind, how easily She was able to adjust to any situation. This is exactly how we should be as well. If we cannot change our situation for the better, we should be ready to adjust our mindset instead.

Early one evening in India, as Amma was walking towards the stage for bhajans, a small child of about three years old was running along beside Her. Amma called out to this little girl, "Kuruvi." At first when I heard this I thought that must be her name. The next day, when we

She Who Brings the Rain

were again going for bhajans and walking up the ramp, Amma started calling, "Kuruvi, Kuruvi," but this time, it was to two other children.

I thought, 'Wait a minute, these children can't *all* be called Kuruvi.' I discovered that *Kuruvi* means little bird, a sparrow. Amma sees everyone like these little birds, fluttering joyfully around Her.

We create our own reality through our mindset and how we view the world. For Amma, who sees the best in everything and tries to share this vision with us, we are all Her little Kuruvis, Her little sparrows. She is feeding us with pure love and divine wisdom.

Wherever we travel in the world, at the end of the programs, people often comment, "That was the best program ever!" It is quite remarkable to hear this. One might think, 'How can every single program be the best ever?' But Amma has the amazing quality of always bringing out the best in everything.

Upon arriving in New Mexico each year, She usually brings the much-needed rain, gaining the reputation there of 'She who brings the rain.' In cold places, She brings the sunshine.

She inspires so much goodness and blessings everywhere She goes.

Recently, while we were in San Ramon, there was an unusually hot day and all the power went out for a long time. I imagined that people might find this really difficult to manage. Even when we are at the ashram in India, if the electricity goes off, it always comes back again within ten seconds. But in San Ramon the power was off for many hours.

Even though there was a lot of chaos getting everyone settled, still the program went on! A small generator fueled a single light on the stage during bhajans, and the rest of the hall was totally dark.

Amma's form was softly outlined in a faint glow up on the stage. Some people's cell phone batteries had died, so they could not look at them and had no choice but to concentrate on the divine light and devotion Amma was sharing. People felt the darkness compelled their minds to be quiet enough to concentrate on the bhajans and they experienced even more bliss than usual. Everyone felt grateful for the experience, and once again said, "That was the best program ever!"

We cannot control what life will bring to us. However, if we develop an attitude of acceptance, it can help us to invoke the light of Grace to experience the blessings of life wherever we are, even through the difficulties.

While we were in Australia, a man came for the evening program wearing dark sunglasses. I thought to myself that he was looking way too cool like that, wearing sunglasses at night. Then I overheard him talking to someone. He mentioned that he had been blind for fifteen years and had just had an operation on his eyes the day before and could now see again.

He felt it was Amma's grace that his vision had been restored, and declared that it was *such a beautiful world*. He proclaimed that he was going to enjoy seeing the beauty in absolutely everything.

Amma reminds us that it is our attitude that makes all the difference. She says that God shows no partiality to anyone, but when we have a positive attitude behind all our actions, it manifests in our life as God's grace.

The Fragrance of Pure Love

Amma can save us from some suffering, but our mind and intentions have to be genuinely pure to enable us to reach the final state of freedom.

We should understand that everything that happens to us is not to punish us, but is meant to awaken us. The Divine, with infinite wisdom and compassion, is just trying to turn us in the right direction so that we can fully and consciously experience the Truth some day, instead of unconsciously being dragged over the coals through life. Some feel that God is cruel to have created a world of suffering, but others accept their fate, looking only to see the best they can in life.

Only through facing life with a positive outlook can we escape the cycle of karma. Then, we can see things differently. If we can learn from our challenges and from our mistakes, the Divine will allow us to move on to the next lesson, accepting we do not have to come back to that same one again. There will always be something else to learn!

Amma insists, "We have to face everything." If we try to escape situations, they will simply arise again. We have to make the most of every situation that comes and try to do it with a smile on our faces. We must do this lovingly or it becomes like a weed: we cut the top off, but the root is still left growing in the ground and will flourish again. If we bravely accept what comes to us, we can destroy the roots of our deeper habits and negative tendencies that repeatedly rise up to the surface. If we have a positive attitude in everything that we do, our life will surely be blessed.

Chapter 13

From Grass to Milk

Amma sees the good in everything. Through all situations Amma remains humble and shows us true surrender and acceptance. She says, "We think that grass is not so important, but when the cow eats it, it eventually turns into milk to nourish us – so truly *everything* has importance." Amma sees everything with equal vision and love.

One time during a long layover at an airport in Frankfurt, Germany, I took Amma into a lounge to wait for our flight. Most of the chairs were full; the only seats I could find were next to some men drinking beer.

I thought to myself, 'Well, they're not too rowdy looking, not like Australian beer drinkers.' I hoped that maybe they would just have a quick drink and leave, but I totally underestimated the staying power of German beer drinkers. They stayed the entire time.

I felt so bad for offering Amma a seat by those men with their beer drinking language, but Amma did not seem to mind. She simply sat there peacefully. Amma feels at home anywhere in the world. Instead of being distracted by the beer drinkers, She looked out the window at the snow. Amma mentioned how the snow reminded Her of the foam on the ocean waves at Amritapuri. She explained that when She was a child, She would go down to the ocean, and for a few months of the year, the foam from the waves looked exactly like this snow did. She was so happy in Her contemplation and remembrance of the ocean. She showed me that no matter where She is, Amma sees only the positive in everything and always remembers Her foundation of love.

A couple moved into a new neighbourhood. The first morning there, while they were eating breakfast, the young woman saw her neighbour hanging the laundry outside.

"That laundry is not very clean," she said. "She doesn't know how to wash correctly. Perhaps she needs better laundry soap!" Her husband looked on but remained silent. Every time this neighbour would hang her wash out to dry, the young woman made similar comments.

About one month later, the woman was surprised to see nice clean clothes on the line and excitedly remarked to her husband, "George, *look!* She has *finally* learned how to wash correctly. Wow! It's about time! I wonder who taught her?" The husband quietly responded, "Sweetheart, I got up early this morning and cleaned our windows." We often blame others for our mistakes, whereas the problems are due to our own limited vision.

I once read an article from Germany about an elderly man who became annoyed hearing the same tune played over and over again. He decided to call the police to complain. He was angry that his neighbours were playing music at all different hours of the day and night and thought they were purposely trying to annoy him. Upon investigation, the police found that the real culprit was a musical greeting card on his own windowsill. The occasional breeze would blow it open, causing it to play. Things are never as we think they are.

We often want to blame our external surroundings for our troubles, but it is our inner attitude that actually determines our reality. We live in a world of our own creation and it is difficult for us to come out of it. We all experience the world differently.

This is why we need some extra help, the help of a Perfect Master. Their grace is *absolutely necessary* to pull us out of the distorted creation of our own making, so that we can accept and surrender to God's creation.

In Amma's presence it becomes much easier to see the good in everything around us. We were driving home to the ashram one day, excited at returning after being away for a few months, when Amma declared, "We really have everything here!" We all started to add our little bit of the wonderful things available in Amritapuri. Amma said, "It's like a festival every day." Swamiji added, "Yes, we have pujas all the time." The driver started adding his few things, "Yes, we have so many wonderful classes in the ashram." Then I added, "We have pizza and ice cream too!" Amma added, "And our ice cream doesn't have any air in it. Ice cream that you get outside is whipped, so you're actually only getting half the amount of ice cream; the other half is air." Amma excitedly explained, "You only get pure ice cream from this place, as it is totally hand made with devotion and mantras." "Yes! We also have swimming, and Amma's darshan!" we were so excited. We felt like we were coming home to heaven on earth. We are so lucky, because we truly were.

Amma's vision inspires our own. Perfect awareness allows love to flow around us, as it does for Her, no matter where She goes. Yet we just see the outside façade of everything; we only see what we want to see, judging everything with our limited vision. It is hard for us to remember our true essence and our foundation of love when we are stuck in our own minds. But Amma can delve beyond the surface to see the truth, beauty and love dwelling within everything. With effort and Her grace, we may one day be able to see everything in life with a pure vision, just like She does.

Chapter 14

Bowing Down to all of Creation

Finding peace and joy is everyone's goal in life. Whatever we are doing is because we are really striving for that. If we want to see peace in the outside world, then we must first find it within our own minds.

Everything Amma does is intended to help calm the doubting mind that is always troubling us and to give us the optimism needed to be open to grace. Amma knows how little we believe in ourselves, She gives Her guidance and blessings to help us adjust our sails so we can ride through whatever storms may come to us.

One November, a woman desperately wanted to come on tour as a volunteer to spend that special extra time with Amma. She made all the arrangements for her flight, but then fell quite ill.

She was extremely disappointed but was forced to cancel her trip. She kept praying and hoping that Amma would heal her before it was time to get on the plane but this did not happen.

She trusted Amma, so despite her disappointment, she still tried to have a good attitude, even though she could not understand why this had happened. Then she received an email that one of her students had been murdered and his funeral would be on the following day.

When she went to the funeral, she found many of her former students there, without their parents. She ended up crying with them and comforting them all. She could feel the comfort of Amma flowing through her arms as she held the distraught teenagers. She knew it was definitely Amma's grace that caused her to cancel her flight, so she was able to be there for her students when they needed her.

Her heart was with Amma, but her hands were busy with service, just the way Amma must have wanted it to be. Amma moves in such mysterious ways. Sometimes we want our service to be exactly how we want it to be, and nothing else, but God may have different plans for us.

Bowing Down to all of Creation

God has put us where we are supposed to be in the world. Nothing that happens is ever a mistake. Our challenge is to graciously accept God's plan. The literal meaning of *"Thy will be done"* is when we truly can accept whatever comes our way, understanding that it is all a part of the Divine Master plan. Wherever we find ourselves, it is for us to learn something, so we should try to accept it.

Life never really turns out how we think it will, especially spiritual life! There may be lots of difficulties that we have to experience, but Amma reminds us that the strongest, finest steel is made only in the hottest furnace – but we all know how difficult it can be to surrender.

I am repeatedly given the opportunity to surrender with all the babysitting I have to do when sitting behind Amma at public programs. Sometimes I have thought that we really should be charging for this, as Amma's program is the best babysitting service in the world!

I have often declared that this is the only place in the world where a professional program will be conducted with kids crawling all over the stage, laughing, talking, crying or arguing while someone is trying to give a speech or the musicians perform. Depending how naughty they are, I have even resorted to pulling the children's ears in order to keep them quiet!

I had a flash of understanding while sitting with these children one night. It dawned on me why Amma is giving me this opportunity: instead of my doing them a favour by looking after them, these children are really helping to awaken something in me. Amma is trying to awaken the Universal motherhood in me, and in all of us, not only in women who have had children. So this is one gift She is offering me toward my awakening.

Amma deals with everyone on an individual level. She is the catalyst for whatever we need in our life to come to us. It is something spontaneous that happens when we come into contact with a Mahatma. If we can surrender, She will take us to a state of perfection.

What is coming to us is for our blessing alone. Cultivate the humility to receive everything in life as a gift, and it will be a beautiful journey. If we have the innocent eyes of a child, accepting everything and using it all as lessons for growth, then life's journey will be a phenomenal experience.

At one time while boarding a flight with Amma, I handed my boarding pass to the steward as we entered the plane. He jovially asked me, "Now tell me, what is your favourite colour?" I have to admit that I felt slightly annoyed at such a silly question, but he seemed so enthusiastic and he *was* holding my boarding pass.

I thought for a second about what my answer could be, a sarcastic response started to bubble up…but then I just decided to surrender and make him happy, so I replied, "Orange!"

"Yes!!!" he said, "That is the correct answer!" He was very excited that I had answered correctly, so he let me go on my way. Actually, I lied…only to make him happy by telling him what I knew he wanted to hear. *Do you really think orange is my favourite colour?*

When we are able to surrender it feels so good and makes others feel good too. Only then can the Divine flow through us. Amma says that when we bow down, we are not just bowing down to other people, but we are bowing down to the whole of creation.

Challenges are not given to us in life to try and destroy us, but instead to bring out the true potential that lies completely untapped within. We learn more from the difficulties if we see them as tests we are being given to grow, to make our minds strong and pure.

No matter how many problems may arise in life, we should try to find equanimity. Then we will become like a lotus flower growing strong out of the filth and mud. Precious lessons come to us disguised in many different ways. When we learn to surrender to them, the hidden beauty that lies within all of life's circumstances reveals itself.

Chapter 15

Perfect Surrender

Amma says that Mahatmas *can* change our destiny, but if they do so we may not learn the lessons that we need to learn from the experiences that present themselves to us. Mahatmas like Amma are completely surrendered to the will of God: they see everything in its correct place, and our destiny playing out as it should. It is not Amma's way to go against the will of God if we have been given something to suffer for a reason – ultimately all of our experiences are meant to help us grow.

If Amma were to take away everything due to come to us, we might turn around and make the same mistakes all over again. We should try to absorb the essence of the teachings that present themselves to us through difficult experiences in life. These experiences arrive, especially tailor made for us, by the Divine will.

I once read an amazing story about a female neuroscientist whose life was totally changed through her experience of having a stroke. One day she was suddenly struck down with a massive brain clot in the left hemisphere of her brain, but she was still able, in the midst of the suffering, to have the awareness of what was happening to her.

Her field of study is how the brain works, so she was able to set herself aside from the experience and totally be the witness to it while suffering from it. She could see her body going through all the symptoms: terrible pain, headaches, loss of feeling in her arm. Thanks to her training and awareness she could watch how her brain worked at the same time.

She stepped outside of the left hemisphere of her brain into the right one and had an out-of-body experience, completely leaving her normal consciousness. This experience showed her the wonder of the universe which can be seen and felt when we are able to escape from the confines of our body and mind.

We tend to build up a barrier and think, 'This is me' and everything else is *not* me. At that time this woman was able to transcend that limited vision and she became one with everything. She had an amazing adventure, seeing the beauty of every atom of the cosmos and how it is made. She kept on going back into the body and feeling the physical symptoms of the stroke, but she was able to get outside of that experience as well.

This stroke was such a positive, mind-blowing event in her life. For a little while she was able to go beyond her little 'self,' filled with all its problems, to experience the exquisite beauty of the larger 'Self,' and truly know what it is like to become one with the Universe. For her to have this realization in the midst of suffering a stroke is almost unbelievable.

It changed her life completely. She could understand the possibilities that exist for all of us. She was a scientist, not a spiritual person, but whether we consider ourselves to be spiritual or not is irrelevant. The path towards understanding the meaning of our lives is for everyone.

We have lived without true awareness for most of our lives and it has become a habit to exist in this way. The majority of people live blindly, ignoring the true potential of what can be achieved with our human birth.

Amma reminds us that we all have the capacity to reach the pinnacle of human existence by opening up the closed bud of our heart.

There is nothing wrong with asking Amma to help us, to pray for what we want, what we need or even to pray about what we feel is unfair in life. We can freely pray for anything – but ultimately we have to become detached from it. As long as we remain attached to all the mental images we build up in our minds, we cannot experience the world as it really is.

Amma feels so much compassion for the sorrows of the world that She will always give Her utmost support in thoughts, words and deeds, to try to make us strong enough to bear what we have to, even though She will not take *all* the suffering away.

A devotee from Switzerland shared a story with me that demonstrated this truth. She said,

> "Ten years ago I had a fatty tumour in my back. When it grew, I asked Mother what to do and She recommended that I ask the doctor. When I went to the

Doctor he told me I needed surgery, as the tumour was possibly malignant.

I was not really afraid. I doubted I actually had cancer and knew I had Mother's protection. I trusted Amma and firmly believed whatever would happen was only for my benefit.

I scheduled the operation for after Amma's visit to Europe so that I could get Her blessing for the surgery. When Mother was in Switzerland, I explained everything and She was extremely affectionate and sweet to me. She caressed my tumour and asked my husband how we will organize taking care of our two children. She is the best Mother in the world and the best friend I've ever had.

In Munich, just a few days before the operation, I went for darshan. Amma looked deeply into my eyes. She asked for my telephone number and if it was okay to call after the procedure to find out how it went. I was overwhelmed by Her compassion and care for me. Tears rolled down my cheeks.

The Fragrance of Pure Love

After the operation, the doctor called my husband and told him that everything had gone well, but there was a high chance the tumour was malignant as it had infiltrated the muscles around it.

When I heard that it might be cancer, I was shocked. I struggled with Mother inside of my head, asking, 'Why do I have to go through all this? What will happen to my children if I die? Why did you forsake me?'

I felt Amma's presence come into my hospital room and sit down on the bed beside me. I felt flooded by Her love and peace. Finally, I surrendered to the possibility of cancer and remembered that everything is for my benefit alone.

After a week I got the test results. The doctor came to my room, seeming a little confused. He mentioned the test had an incredible outcome: the tumour was benign, but he didn't believe it. He wanted to test it again and let me know the results. I just smiled and felt Mother sitting beside me. The results of the second test came back: no cancer. I was allowed to go home to my family.

When I thanked Amma for saving my life, She humbly replied, "It was God's grace that the tumour changed."

We have to be strong to face everything that comes to us, realizing that challenges in our life are always a blessing in disguise, meant to enable our growth. If we can remember this, the journey will become easier for us. Yet, we usually fight against everything that comes to us, believing it is someone else's fault, not right or unfair!

If we resist everything, we will always have to suffer. God does not give us pain to punish us. It manifests to open our hearts, so that we may understand more deeply who we truly are. If we learn to accept – then we too might be able one day, to embody the perfect surrender we are so attracted to in Amma. She accepts the flow of life with all of its surprises. It is this acceptance that allows Divine grace to enter.

Chapter 16

The Flow of Grace

Grace will always carry us through when we need it the most. It is the added factor that makes our lives sweet and helps us to rise above *all* difficulties. Optimism is what allows grace to enter.

The rare flow of grace that comes from a living Mahatma can truly change our lives. Amma's grace is constantly flowing to every one of us. It is not that Amma loves some people more than others; some just find a way to open up their hearts to tune into grace, while others put up an umbrella that shields them from the flow. Wherever you may find yourself, understand that Amma is beyond the cosmic law of time and space. Her grace can flow to you wherever you may be.

God's grace will always find us when we lead a life of devotion. Amma has sincerely promised that our heartfelt prayers will reach Her. We can have a direct connection with Her. The phone line is never busy if we send those prayers direct – and there is no charge at all in that cosmic communication system.

Here is one story that illustrates the blossoming of grace so beautifully: a young girl finished school and asked Amma what she should do with her life. Amma told her she should study medicine and invited her to study at the medical college at AIMS in India. This girl was totally surprised, as she had not excelled academically and also had a major disability. She had an eye disease that made it extremely difficult to read. Knowing how much study is required to learn medicine, she never would have imagined that she could do it.

Still, Amma insisted that she try, so with full faith, she surrendered and enrolled in the medical college at AIMS.

Most of us who knew the girl were doubtful that she could succeed, realizing all the years of complex study needed, but somehow she managed to pass her way through every year.

When the final exams came, in her class of thirty students, the person that everyone had *thought* would be at the top of the class, the one who usually got the highest marks, ended up failing the exams. Contrary to all of her and everyone else's expectations, *this* girl, with the eye problem, received a very high grade, rising to the top five of her class.

I was amazed when she related that out of the whole class, the six students who were devotees of Amma ended up receiving the top six grades with honours. The one with the lowest attendance, because of travelling with Amma, received the very highest mark of distinction.

By this example I am not saying if you become devoted to Amma you will not have to study, but one should at least be aware of the miraculous and unfathomable power of grace that can unfold in our lives, if we open up and allow it to flow through us.

Making the necessary effort at the beginning is the important thing, because otherwise it is very difficult for God's grace to enter. Once we have made our best effort, we must simply trust in grace to guide us through. When we surrender and tune our minds to Amma, grace simply manifests.

Effort is essential in opening to grace. Amma gives the example: if we are going on a road journey in the mountains, we should check the car's engine and brakes first, to see they are working properly. We should make sure there is enough petrol, oil and water in the engine, and that our windshield is clean. After we have done all these things, trying our maximum to make sure everything is in order, we must leave the rest to God's grace.

A devotee in California has a teenage son with a very rare medical condition that left him with the undeveloped mind of a child. He used to sit on the couch with his mother every day, while year after year she would try to teach him how to read. By the time he reached age fifteen, she was concerned he might never learn.

At her wit's end this mother came to Amma and begged Her to help. Amma told her to bring a sandalwood stick for blessing. The mother obtained one and went for darshan with her son. The boy grabbed the sandalwood from his mother's hand and gave it to Amma himself, looking deeply into Her eyes. His mother was so surprised by her son's behaviour, as he usually never looked at anyone directly. Amma gazed back at him and returned the sandalwood stick after blessing it.

He applied the sandalwood paste on his forehead every day, and amazingly started to learn how to read. Two years later his mother informed me that he now reads five hundred page books which he borrows from the library. He also reads the newspaper every day. He scrutinizes the newspaper columns and then writes to governors to save people from death row. He works for peace and justice, one letter at a time. His mother says that her son now knows much more about politics than she does.

This child will always remain developmentally challenged, but with a heart of gold from Amma's blessings, he knows his dharmic path to follow.

We are so blessed that we have the guiding light of a great soul like Amma to shine hope on our path, showing us the way to walk safely through this crazy world in these difficult times. We should always try to hold onto hope, even when we believe that the whole world is turning against us. Try to earn that magnificent grace of the Guru, however you can. All it takes is to make the right effort and to develop the right mindset.

Chapter 17

Guiding Our Footsteps

Amma proves to us in all sorts of ways that She is always with us. She goes to endless lengths with Her care and protection. No matter where we may go in the world, She is looking over us with a Divine love that will never abandon us.

A woman came to me in Australia and told me an almost unbelievable story. She had wanted to buy her daughter some sort of amulet to keep her safe on an upcoming journey to South America. She decided to get her daughter a rudraksha bead anklet that had been worn by Amma.

Unfortunately, on the trip her daughter fell extremely sick in a very small village. She did not understand the local language and had no one with her to help her. Noticing she was sick, one of the local village women approached her. She saw the anklet on the girl's leg and gestured to it. Pointing at it, she asked, "Amma?" Although they could not understand each other's language they discovered a word that created a universal bond between them.

The woman took the girl home with her. The girl was amazed and grateful to find a photo of Amma on the wall of the small village house. This woman had met Amma and had Her darshan at one of the programs in Chile. A photo of Amma's feet was displayed prominently in the entrance to her home.

She nursed the young girl back to health. This girl later phoned her mother to convey the story; she felt Amma had really saved her life and had so sweetly given protection in a time of need.

We have the presence of the greatest, most compassionate enlightened Master who has ever lived on this Earth. She offers us Her protection and the cool breeze of Her Grace, in the middle of the desert of life. Even when times and situations seem difficult, She protects us. Maybe we have to suffer a little. That may just be our destiny, but Amma offers Her shade to everyone. It is always there. She promises that.

A devotee wrote this story about her experience with Amma:

"The year was 2007, it was late spring and I was preparing to see Amma in Puyallup, near Seattle, for Her darshan.

I was so excited that day because my best friend had called and said he wanted to attend the program with me. This friend had never been interested in meeting Amma before. For years I had been asking him to come, sometimes even pleading with him; but he had always resisted going to see Her. I had taken a picture of him to Amma the year before in order to ensure that he received Amma's blessings but I never told him that I did this. Immediately following this, he changed his mind and decided to go to see Amma. That was the first small miracle.

Anyway, there I was getting dressed and feeling very happy to be taking him with me for the first time. On the drive down the highway to pick him up I found myself ecstatic with joy and gratitude. Waves of bliss swept over me and tears trailed down my face. I had to focus very hard in order to concentrate on the road.

I reached his home and we headed out to Puyallup. I was driving in the fast lane wanting to get to the event as soon as possible. All of a sudden my car stopped running. I watched the odometer fall. The steering wheel and brakes stopped responding. I had no power. There was a lot of traffic on the road that day, but somehow the car crossed all four lanes of traffic safely and stopped on the shoulder of the road. I can't explain how a car that had lost all power and should have stopped dead managed to cross all that traffic, but it did. That is the miracle of Amma's grace. She saved our lives that day.

Once we caught our breath and stopped looking around in amazement, I tried turning on the ignition and heard a horrible sound from the engine. We got out of the car and opened the hood to find that the engine had caught on fire. The fire had put itself out, but the engine was still smoking and the hood was badly burnt.

What to do? We were stranded on the freeway with a car that wasn't going anywhere that day. We called for help and I had the car towed back to my friend's home. He thought maybe it was a sign that we weren't supposed to go see Amma but I wouldn't hear of it. I told him that he simply needed to drive us, because we absolutely had to go.

We arrived late to the darshan hall but were nonetheless provided with tokens. To my surprise and delight the tokens were an early number, which meant we were able to see Amma relatively quickly.

While I was in Amma's arms a group of devotees started singing. One of the singers performed a solo singing (off key) with such devotion, that Amma listened in rapture to the whole song. She held me in Her arms the entire time, rocking me and laughing. All worries and concerns were lifted from my shoulders. It became clear as She held and comforted me that She knew exactly what had happened to us. It was the longest darshan I have ever had.

My friend had his darshan next and was completely moved by his experience with Amma.

I truly feel that Amma saved our lives that afternoon. There is no question in my mind that it was Amma's grace that guided our car to safety that night. As I write these words my eyes are filled with tears. Amma has consistently over the years looked out for me, guided me and has been my constant companion. I will forever remain in Her lap. She is my very breath, and has all my soul's love and devotion."

All it takes is a little effort and faith and we will begin to see Amma's gentle hand guiding our every footstep. We have to cultivate the faith that a Higher level of Divinity is in fact guiding us safely through all events, because in truth, She is.

Chapter 18

Cultivating Innocent Faith

When we watch Amma, it is important that we do not judge Her by what we perceive Her to be doing. It is best to simply accept Her actions, knowing they are always for the best. Whatever She does is only for *our* benefit. We dwell in this realm of three dimensions, but Amma's consciousness dwells in another place entirely. Who knows how many dimensions there are?

Once some atomic scientists asked Her, "Can You explain to us about creation?" She replied, "Creation takes place on a higher dimension. You only dwell in three dimensions so your mind is not able to reach beyond that to understand." We do not need to understand, we just have to have faith and trust.

Making the conscious effort to develop faith in someone like Amma, is an act so pure, it will draw an inconceivable amount of blessings to us in this life. We have to develop a strong faith that Amma hears all our prayers. We have so much faith in lesser things in our lives, believing many foolish people who tell us silly things. Try to have the understanding that Amma does hear our prayers, our desires and our wishes. We can totally connect with Her when we make a bond of love with Her – for pure Love knows no distance.

One lady told me she had always doubted that Amma really wanted or needed her. There were always a lot of people in the crowds and this woman questioned if Amma would really miss her if she was not there. She decided to test Amma. She thought to herself, 'If Amma really wants me here, She will make me stay for the program.'

When no sign came for her to stay, she decided, 'Oh well…let me go to the car; I'm going. Amma didn't give me a sign.'

She went out to the car and tried to start it, but she could not start the car and was totally annoyed. Why didn't the car start? She was stuck there, having already forgotten that she had asked Amma for a sign. She surrendered to the fact she was trapped at the program for the evening.

At the end of the night she thought, 'It's time for me to leave. Let me just check and see if the car starts.' She went to the car again, turned on the engine and it started straight away, allowing her to travel home without any trouble. It was only some time later that she realized, when testing Amma, the answer had appeared in a way she just *never* imagined it would.

We want the whole universe to come to us in a way that our little mind expects it to – but things rarely work like that.

When someone has proven themselves to us, like Amma has, it is time to stop our doubting; because only She really knows what is correct, what is true and what we need. It is for us to try to bow down and surrender our ego and not judge through our distorted vision.

Amma explains, through this delightful anecdote, the kind of faith we need to cultivate in order to hear the Master's voice clearly within us.

In a certain village, there had been a drought for a very long time. There was absolutely no rain at all. The villagers decided to perform a ritual to invoke the rains. On the evening of the ritual, thousands of people gathered to take part in the event. Among all the thousands of people attending, there was just one little girl who had brought an umbrella along with her. Some people asked her, "Why have you brought an umbrella along with you on such a clear day?"

The girl replied, "Well, after the ritual it is going to rain, right? I brought it so that I won't get wet." Even though the sun was shining brightly, she definitely believed that it would rain. The child carried an umbrella because there was not a doubt in her mind that the ritual would work. Only this child had complete innocent faith, which is the kind of faith that a disciple needs to develop.

It is through faith that we awaken the strength and potential inside of us. Faith allows us to develop our self-confidence – confidence in one's true Self. This Self-belief helps us to grow

www.ingramcontent.com/pod-product-compliance
Lightning Source LLC
Chambersburg PA
CBHW061955070426
42450CB00011BA/3048